CONTENTS

1

SECTION 1

All prime numbers are greater than 1

5^2 means 5×5

SKIPS™

SKIPS™ CHALLENGE TIME!

Well Done! Now that you have completed the crossmaths, it is SKIPS™ Challenge Time. Copy the numbers from each of the coloured boxes in the crossmaths to the matching coloured boxes below. Then add up all the numbers and you will have a square number.

What is the square number? = ☐ __ __

☐ + ☐ + ☐ ☐ + ☐ + ☐ + ☐ + ☐ + ☐ + ☐ + ☐ + ☐ - ☐ - ☐

NUMBERS

ACROSS

1   What is the lowest prime number?
2   The next prime number bigger than 50?
3   What is 4^2 (i.e 4 squared)?
5   The last even number before 100?
6   What is 5^3 (i.e 5 cubed)?
9   Calculate $5^2 + 6^2 - 3^3 =$
10 A cube number between 81 and 140?
12 What do the factors of 24 all add up to?
15 A prime number between 82 and 87?
16 What is $11^2 = ?$
18 What is four squared plus six squared?
19 What is the lowest square number?
20 What is $5^2 = ?$
21 What is half between one hundred and two hundred?
25 What do the factors of 18 add up to?
26 What is the square root of 49?
27 Which number is half way between 18 and 30?
28 The next prime number bigger than 20?

DOWN

4   What is the next prime number bigger than 54?
7   What do the factors of 15 add up to?
8   How many factors does 24 have?
9   Calculate $2^2 + 3^3 = ?$
11 What is the last prime number before 100?
12 What is the next cube number higher than 36?
13 What is the next highest square number after 77?
14 What is the next prime number after 7?
17 What is the last odd number before 25?
20 What is the last square number before 33?
22 A number that is both a square and a cube number?
23 What is twenty four add six?
24 Calculate the square root of 81.

The HINTS are there to help you...read them through from time to time.

HINTS

A prime number can only have two factors, which is 1 and itself.

All prime numbers are greater than 1

When a number multiplies by itself, it gives a square number, e.g.
6^2 means 6 squared which is 6 x 6

Cube number is the answer when a number multiplies by itself three times, i.e. 27 (cube number) = 3 x 3 x 3

A factor is what we call a number that goes into (divides) another number without leaving a remainder.

The square root of a number is a value that when multiplied by itself equals the given number.
E.g. The square root of 9 is 3, because when 3 is multiplied by itself you get 9.

Remember to use the **HINTS** to help as you work through the crossmaths.

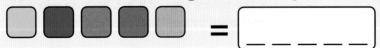

PLACE VALUE

ACROSS

1 Which digit has the value of tenths in 7.652?
2 Round 0.1284 to 1 decimal place.
4 Calculate 277.95 + 128.60 =
5 Calculate 159.94 + 150.12 =
10 Which digit has a value of hundredths in 110.356?
11 Round 45.44 to the nearest whole number.
13 Round 8.346 to 2 decimal places.
15 Which digit has a value of tenths in 10.524?
16 Round 1034 to the nearest hundred.
18 What is 2.1416 rounded to 2 decimal places?
19 What is 1.094 rounded to 1 decimal place?

DOWN

1 Calculate 421.35 + 194.71. (Answer to 1 decimal place).
3 Round 1.895 to 2 decimal places.
4 Calculate 282.66 – 242.01 =
5 Calculate 341.09 + 10.92 =
6 Which digit has a value of units in 5.89?
7 Which digit has a value of thousandths in 3.285?
8 Which digit has a value of units in 4.361?
9 Calculate 534.65 – 417.33 =
12 Write the value of the unit in 7.6
14 What is 160.014 rounded to 2 decimal places?
17 What is 10.74 rounded to the nearest whole number?
20 Which number has a value of hundredths in 0.014?

HINTS

Every Digit in a Number has a Place Value.
Before a decimal the place values are known as: Thousands (Th), Hundreds (H), Tens (T), Units (U).

The place value after a decimal are Tenths ($\frac{1}{10}$ ths), Hundredths ($\frac{1}{100}$ ths) and Thousandths ($\frac{1}{1000}$ ths).

E.g: Take a look at the number 2143.145 below.

Th	H	T	U	.	$\frac{1}{10}$	$\frac{1}{100}$	$\frac{1}{1000}$
2	1	4	3	.	1	4	5

What Is Rounding?
Rounding means reducing the digits in a number whilst trying to keep the value similar.

Common Method:
1) Decide which is the last digit to keep.
2) Leave it the same if the next digit is less than '5'.
3) Increase it by '1' if the next digit is '5' or more.

E.g. Round 0.1274 to 2 decimal places:
This is the second decimal number
↓
0.1274
↑
This is the third decimal number

Solution:
The third decimal number, '7' which is greater than '5', so we add '1' and drop the rest of the decimal numbers:
Answer: 0.13 i.e. 0.1274 = 0.13 (2dp)

Read through HINTS first, they will help you to understand fractions.

SKIPS™ CHALLENGE TIME!

Well Done! Now copy the numbers from the coloured boxes in the crossmaths into the matching coloured boxes below and answer the following questions:

A) ▢ + ▢ − ▢ − ▢ = [ ]

B) ▢ $\dfrac{▢}{▢}$ ÷ $\dfrac{▢}{▢}$ = [ ]

You're doing well

FRACTIONS

ACROSS

1 What fraction of this shape is NOT shaded?

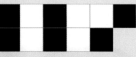

2 What fraction of this shape IS shaded?

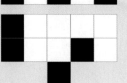

3 Calculate $\frac{17}{22} - \frac{9}{22}$

4 What is $\frac{46}{88}$ reduced to its lowest term?

9 What is the highest common factor of 24 and 8

10 Calculate $\frac{8}{10} - \frac{2}{5}$

14 Calculate $12 \div \frac{1}{2}$

15 Calculate $\frac{7}{36} \div \frac{7}{18}$

17 What is the lowest common multiple of 3 & 10?

18 30 out of 50 reduced to its lowest term?

19 Calculate $\frac{30}{40} - \frac{1}{4}$

24 Reduce $\frac{33}{66}$ reduced to its lowest term.

25 Write $2\frac{1}{2}$ as an improper fraction.

DOWN

5 Calculate $\frac{10}{11} - \frac{12}{22}$

6 Calculate $\frac{1}{3} \div \frac{6}{11}$

7 What is the highest common factor of 18 and 24.

8 Calculate $\frac{10}{11} \times \frac{1}{2}$

11 Calculate $\frac{15}{18} - \frac{1}{6}$

12 Calculate $\frac{2}{3} \times \frac{1}{2}$

13 Calculate $\frac{13}{22} - \frac{2}{11}$

16 Reduce $\frac{18}{66}$ to its lowest term.

20 What is 45 out of 90 as a fraction reduced to its lowest term?

21 What fraction has been shaded in to its lowest term?

22 Calculate $\frac{3}{4} - \frac{2}{8}$

23 Calculate $4\frac{1}{4} \times \frac{1}{11}$

HINTS

Factors are the numbers you multiply together to get another number: e.g.
6 x 4 = 24 (factors are 6 and 4).
The factors of 24 are: 1, 2, 3, 4, 6, 8, 12 and 24.

Improper fractions can be changed to mixed numbers when the bottom number divides into the top number to give a whole number and a fraction as a remainder. e.g. $\frac{14}{5} = 2\frac{4}{5}$

The top part of the fraction is called a <u>numerator.</u>
The bottom part of a fraction is called a <u>denominator.</u>
Before you can add or subtract fractions, the fractions need to have a common denominator. Look for the lowest common denominator. (L.C.D). e.g.

$\frac{1}{3} + \frac{2}{5} = \frac{5}{15} + \frac{6}{15} = \frac{5+6}{15} = \frac{11}{15}$

Simplify / Reducing Fractions - Divide the top and bottom by the highest number (Highest Common Factor, H.C.F)that can divide into both numbers exactly until we can't go on anymore. The top and bottom of the fraction must always be a whole number. You can only multiply or divide, never add or subtract, to get an equivalent fraction. e.g. simplify: $\frac{75}{225} = \frac{3}{9} = \frac{1}{3}$

When multiplying fractions we multiply the <u>numerators</u> with each other and multiply the <u>denominators</u> with each other.
e.g. $\frac{1}{2} \times \frac{3}{4} = \frac{1 \times 3}{2 \times 4} = \frac{3}{8}$

To divide fractions one simply inverts the second fraction and then multiply like before.
e.g. $\frac{3}{4} \div \frac{1}{2} = \frac{3}{4} \times \frac{2}{1}$ (inverted) $= \frac{6}{4}$

reduced: $\frac{6}{4} = \frac{3}{2} = 1\frac{1}{2}$

7

E.g. $\frac{3}{4} = \frac{75}{100} = 0.75$

Step 1) Find a number you can multiply so that the bottom of the fraction will make 10, or 100, or 1000, or any 1 followed by 0's.

Step 2) Multiply both top and bottom by that number.

Step 3) Then write down just the top number, putting the decimal point in the correct place (one space from the right hand side for every zero in the bottom number).

E.g. $0.625 = \frac{0.625}{1} = \frac{625}{1000} = \frac{25}{40} = \frac{5}{8}$

Step 1) Write down the decimal divided by 1

Step 2) Multiply both top and bottom by 10 for every number after the decimal point. (For example: if there are two numbers after the decimal point, use 100, if there are three use 1000, etc. Here we have three numbers after the decimal point so multiply top and bottom by 1000.

Step 3) Simplify (reduce) this fraction.

FRACTIONS

E.g. $\frac{1}{4} = \frac{1}{4} \times \frac{100}{1} = \frac{100}{4} = 25\%$

Step 1) Multiply fraction by $\frac{100}{1}$

Step 2) Multiply across / Reduce

Step 3) Add the % sign

www.skipscrosswords.co.uk

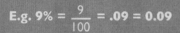

E.g. 9% = $\frac{9}{100}$ = .09 = 0.09

Step 1) 9% means 9 out of 100

Step 2) Divide by 100
(Move decimal point two places to the left).

E.g. 0.14 = 0.14 x 100 = 014. = 14%

Step 1) Multiply by 100 (move decimal point two places to the right)

Step 2) Add percentage sign %

PERCENTAGES

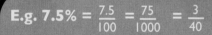

E.g. 7.5% = $\frac{7.5}{100}$ = $\frac{75}{1000}$ = $\frac{3}{40}$

Step 1) Create a fraction by placing the decimal number as the top part and the 100 as the bottom of the fraction.

Step 2) Move decimal point to the end of the number on top part and for every positioned move add a 0 to the number underneath.

Step 3) Simplify /Cancel

RT FOR DECIMALS

www.skipscrosswords.co.uk

Decimal, Fraction & Percentage are different ways of saying the same value

$\frac{3}{4}$
as a percentage
$=\frac{3}{4} \times \frac{100}{1}$
= 75%

Don't forget to check the HINTS!

SKIPS™ CHALLENGE TIME!
Well Done! Now copy the numbers from the coloured boxes in the crossmaths into the matching coloured boxes below and answer the following questions:

A) ☐.☐☐☐ + ☐.☐☐☐ = ☐_._☐☐

B) ☐.☐☐☐ - ☐.☐☐☐ - ☐ = ☐_.☐☐☐

That's great

Fractions, Decimals, Percentages

ACROSS

1 Which digit has a value of thousandths in 3.285?

2 Write one twentieth as a fraction.

4 Write this fraction as a decimal: $\frac{748}{1000}$

7 What is 12% of 75?

11 What is $\frac{2}{25}$ as a percentage?

12 What is $\frac{4}{80}$ as a percentage?

13 What is 0.08 as a percentage?

14 Which digit has a value of units in 2.7?

15 Write $\frac{16}{40}$ as a percentage.

16 Write the decimal 0.12 as a percentage.

17 Write $\frac{420}{100}$ as a decimal.

20 Write $1\frac{1}{10}$ as a decimal.

23 Write $8\frac{3}{5}$ as a decimal to 1 decimal place.

25 What is 50% as a fraction in its lowest term?

26 Write $\frac{18}{40}$ as a percentage.

27 Which digit has the value of tenths in 4.91?

DOWN

3 Write the value of 3 in 9.143 as a fraction.

4 Write this fraction as a decimal, $\frac{1}{1000}$

5 Write $8\frac{33}{100}$ as a decimal.

6 Write 0.04 as a percentage.

8 What is 10% of 30?

9 Write 0.6 as a fraction in its lowest form.

10 Write 70% as a decimal to 2 decimal places.

17 Write the fraction $4\frac{7}{10}$ as a decimal to 1 decimal place.

18 Write $\frac{1}{5}$ as a percentage.

19 Write the fraction $\frac{18}{100}$ as a decimal.

21 What is 10% of 12?

22 What is 5 % of 200?

24 What is 0.99 - 0.29? (Answer to 1 decimal place).

HINTS

Decimals, Fractions & Percentages are different ways of showing the same value. When we write numbers, the position (or 'place') of each number is important, 'Place Value'.

A percentage is a top part of a fraction whose bottom number is 100. e.g. $\frac{1}{2} = \frac{50}{100} = 50\%$

Decimal Numbers are Whole Numbers plus Tenths, Hundredths, Thousandths, etc.

When adding or subtracting decimals write down the numbers, one under the other, with the decimal points lined up. Put in zeros so the numbers have the same length. Then add normally, remembering to put the decimal point in the answer.

When multiplying decimals multiply normally, ignoring the decimal points. Then put the decimal point in the answer - it will have as many decimal places as the two original numbers combined. e.g 0.04 x 1.1
Multiply without decimal point 4 x 11 = 44
Now 0.04 has 2 decimal places and 1.1 has 1 decimal place.
So the answer has to have 3 decimal places: 0.044
When dividing use long division (ignoring the decimal point). Then put the decimal point in the same spot as the number being divided.
E.g. 9.1 ÷ 7
We now have, ignoring the decimal point $7\overline{)91}$ ^{13}
Put the decimal point in the answer directly above the decimal point in the number that has been divided.
$7\overline{)9.1}$ $^{1.3}$ The answer is 1.3

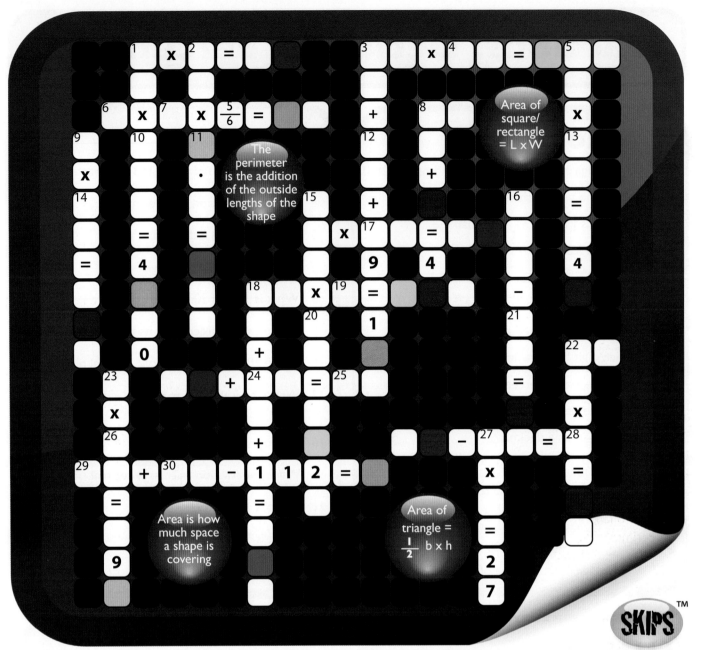

It will help you to memorise the HINTS in the crossmaths

SKIPS™ CHALLENGE TIME!

Well Done! Now copy the numbers from the coloured boxes in the crossmaths into the matching coloured boxes below and answer the following questions:

A) What is the area of the triangle?

= _____ m²

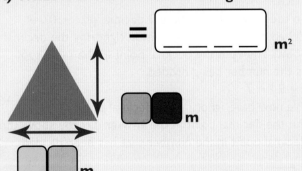

⬜⬜ m

B) The perimeter of a rectangle is

⬛⬛ cm

The length of a rectangle is ⬜⬜ cm

1) What is the width of the rectangle?

= _____ cm

2) What is the area of the rectangle?

= _____ cm²

12

www.skipscrosswords.co.uk

Perimeters, Areas, Compound Shapes

ACROSS

1 The rectangle has area 12mm². What is length x?

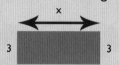

2 What is the missing width for this rectangle, which has an area of 36mm²?

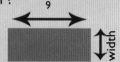

3 What is the perimeter of the rectangle?

4 What is the perimeter of a square that has an edge length of 8m?

From the shape below answer the following:

6 What is height H?
7 Base B length?
8 Perimeter of compound shape?

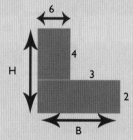

17 What is the perimeter of a rectangle that has sides length 11m and width 10m?

If a rectangle has a perimeter of 38m and a width of 11m, what is:

18 The area of the shape?
19 The length of the rectangle?

From this shape what is:

22 Area of B?
24 Area of A?
25 Total area of the shape?

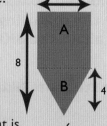

From the shape below what is

27 The total perimeter?
28 Area A?
29 Area B?
30 The total area?

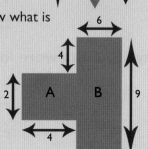

DOWN

1 What is the perimeter of a square that has a side length of 11m?
2 What is the area of the triangle?

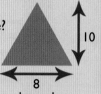

3 What is the area of a triangle that has a base length of 7m and height of 8m?
5 What is the area of a square that has a side 8mm?
8 What is the area of a triangle that has height 8cm and base 8cm?
9 What is the length of a square that has an area of 64m²?
10 What is the area of a square that is 10 m wide?
11 If the area of a triangle is 25mm² and has a base length of 20mm. What is the height of the triangle?
12 What is the area of a square that is 9m wide?
13 What is the height of a triangle that has a base length of 6cm and an area of 30cm²?

From the following shape what is:

14 Area of A?
15 Area of B?
16 Total area of shape?

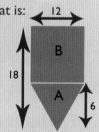

From the following shape what is:

18 Area of A?
20 Area of B?
21 Total area?

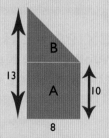

22 What is the measurement of the base for a triangle that has an area 10m² and height 2m?

From the shape below what is:

23 Area A?
24 Perimeter?
26 Total area?

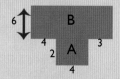

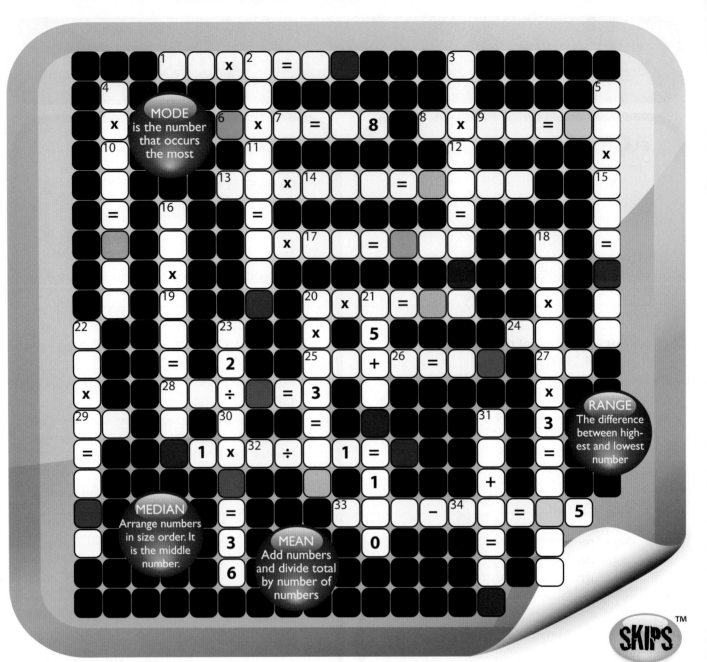

The big challenge

SKIPS™ CHALLENGE TIME!

Well Done! Now copy the numbers from the coloured boxes in the crossmaths into the matching coloured boxes below and answer the following questions:

The Venn diagram shows what students thought about the SKIPS Educational books.

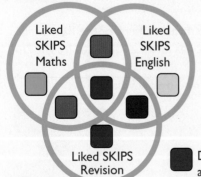

Liked SKIPS Maths

Liked SKIPS English

Liked SKIPS Revision

Did not like any of the books

A) How many students liked all the books?

=

B) How many students were in the class?

= __ __

Fantastic

14

ACROSS

1   What is the range of these numbers:
    1, 6, 7, 12, 1, 1, 6?

2   Find the mode of these numbers:
    9, 2, 9, 6, 9, 2, 8, 7, 4, 2, 9.

6   What is the mean, 6, 8, 9, 1, 7, 6, 10, 4, 3, 6?

7   What is the missing number if the mean for the
    following numbers is ten: 11, 14, 7, 6, 14, ...?

8   What is the missing number if the mean for the
    following numbers is eight: 11, 5, 7, 12, ...?

9   What is the range of the following numbers:
    27, 31, 24, 39, 31, 36?

13 What is the mean of these numbers:
    25, 45, 10, 15, 5?

14 What is the mode of the following numbers:
    117, 125, 136, 124, 125, 116, 125?

17 If there are 135 blue marbles and 24 red
    marbles in a bag, what is the missing ratio in its
    lowest term?
    Blue marbles : red marbles = ? : 8

These are the subjects children liked at
school. Use the instruction given to fill in the
Venn diagram......and answer the following:

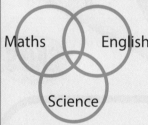

9 children liked Maths
6 children liked English
2 children liked Science
8 liked Maths & English
3 liked Maths & Science
7 liked English & Science
4 children liked all subjects

24 How many children liked English?
25 How many children didn't like Maths?
26 How many different subjects are there?
27 How many children didn't like English?
28 How many children liked Maths?
29 How many children were in the group?
32 In a zoo there are 72 lions and 8 elephants.
    What is the missing ratio of lions to elephants
    in its lowest term. ...... : 1?
33 Peter scores 40 runs in a cricket match. The
    ratio of Peter's score to Mark's score was
    2 : 5. What was Mark's score?
34 Simon saved £35. The ratio of Simon's savings to
    his brother John was 7 : 5. How much did John
    save?

DOWN

2   Find the mode of these numbers:
    102, 99, 84, 84, 101, 99, 85, 99,

3   Find the range of these numbers:
    8, 5, 11, 10, 1

4   Find the mean of these numbers:
    1, 7, 3, 10, 3, 8, 8, 8

5   Find the range of these numbers:
    8, 2, 11, 11, 17, 11
    The chart shows a students mark in four exams.
    Write down the score for each subject.

    10) English =
    11) Science =
    12) Maths =
    15) History =

16 If there are 30 oranges and 2 apples in a fruit
    bowl, what is the missing ratio in its lowest
    term. Oranges : Apples = ... : 1?

The Venn diagram shows what people were
wearing.

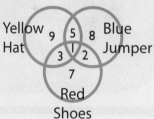

18 How many people were wearing a yellow hat?
19 How many were not wearing a blue jumper?
20 How many were wearing a yellow hat and red
    shoes?
21 How many people were wearing a yellow hat
    and blue jumper but not red shoes?
22 How many people were there altogether?
23 How many people were only wearing red
    shoes?
30 What is the missing amount if you divide 36 in
    the ratio 1 : 5 = ... : 30?
31 What is the missing amount if 100 is divided in
    the ratio 7 : 3 = ... : 30?

15

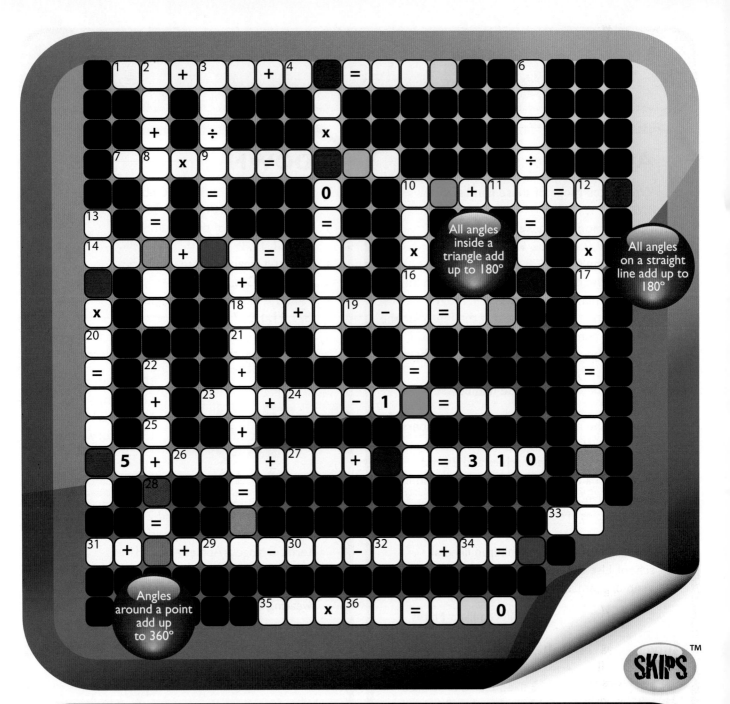

ANGLES

ACROSS

Work out the missing angles of these triangles

	1st angle	2nd angle	3rd angle
1	45°	90°	?
3	80°	20°	?
4	35°	70°	?
7	65°	50°	?
9	110°	15°	?
10	81°	?	75°
11	?	67°	38°

What are the missing angles of the shapes below?

14   x =

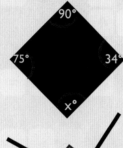

15   x =

The pie chart shows how lazy Nicole spends her day (24 hours). How long does she spend doing the following?

18   Sleeping (s) ....hrs.
19   Playing (p) ....hrs.
20   Lessons (L) ....hrs.
21   Activities(A) ....hrs.

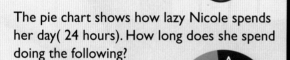

160 Children were asked what their favourite colour was.
20 liked purple best.

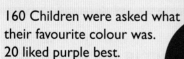

Fill in the table below and put your answer into the crossmaths

Favourite Colour	Fraction of children	Angle of slice	Number of children
Red	22) _	23) _	24) _
Yellow	25) _	26) _	27) _
Blue	28) _	29) _	30) _
Purple	31) _	32) _	33) _
Green	34) _	35) _	36) _

DOWN

What are the missing angles?

2) x =   3) x =

 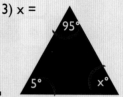

5) x =   6) x =

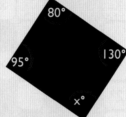 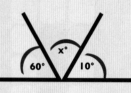

8) x =

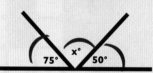

Find the missing angles from the diagrams shown.

10) x =   12) y =

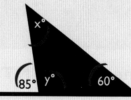

13) x =

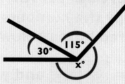

16) x =
17) y =

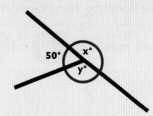

There are some extra HINTS in the crossmaths to help you!

SKIPS™ CHALLENGE TIME!

Well Done! Now copy the numbers from the coloured boxes in the crossmaths into the matching coloured boxes below and answer the following questions:

A) If ▢$_x$ + ▢$_y$ = ▢▢ and y = ▢ , what is the value of x? = ▢

B) Complete the following function machine x

▢ → | add to the product of ▢ and ▢ | → x = ▢

Fun, isn't it?

www.skipscrosswords.co.uk

ACROSS

1 If $a + 2 = 5$ $a = ?$
2 If $d + 9 = 15$ $d = ?$
5 If $x = 4$ what is the value of $2x - 2$?
6 Write ten squared in index notation form.
7 $2a + 10 = 4a + 2$ $a = ?$
8 $3y + 34 = 5y + 4$ $y = ?$
10 If $x = 6$, what is x^2 ?
11 If $x = 3$ and $y = 4$, what is the value of $4x + 5y - 1$?

Complete the function machines by finding the value of x

22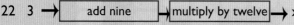
24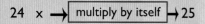
25

26 If $3w - 2 = 2w + 2$, what is the value of w?
31 What is the product of 8 & 2 in index notation?
32 What is the product of three two's?
35 Written in standard format what has the highest value, 2^3, 4^2, 5^2 or 24
36 If $x = 5$ and $y = 24$, what is the value of x^2y?
37 If $2(x + 4) = 3x - 1$, what is value of x?
38 If $2(w + 3) = w + 4^2 + 7$, $w = ...$?

39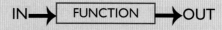
what is the value of x?

DOWN

3 If $w - 3 = 1$, what is w?
4 If $a = 6$, what is the value of a^2?
9 If $5x + 2 = 2x + 14$, what is the value of x?
12 Write two squared in index notation.
13 If $5a + 9 = 6a - 3$, what is a?
14 $2a + 14 = 6a + 2$, what is a?

Complete the following function machines

15
16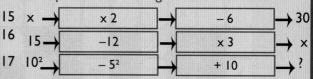
17

18 Write five squared in index notation.
19 If $2(x+1) = 4$, what is the value of x?
20 If $3(x - 4) = 9$, what is value of x?
21 If $8^2 + 6^2 = 2x$, what is value of x?
23 If $3^3 + 20 = x + 5$, what is the value of x?
27 The sum of three numbers is 24. The other two numbers are 6 and 10. What is the value of the third number?
28 Divide the sum of 40 and 20 by four.
29 Write 36 in index notation.
30 Subtract 10 from the product of 9 and 2.
33 Rishi bought some sweets for 35p and some crisps for 80p. How much change did he get from £1.40?
34 Sacha receives 38p change from £2.00 after buying 6 cans of fizzy pop. Find the cost of each can of fizzy pop.

HINTS

In algebra the letters represent numbers and can be written as the following e.g.

$a + a + a = 3a$
$a \times a = a^2$ (not 2a)
$c \times c \times c = c^3$ (not 3c)
$a \times b \times 4 = 4ab$ (put numbers first then letters in alphabetical order)
$x \div y = \dfrac{x}{y}$ (a division is usually written as a fraction)
$3(a+b) = (3 \times a) + (3 \times b) = 3a + 3b$

Re arranging a formula is known as the balancing method. This means whatever you do to one side of the equation, you must do exactly the same to the other side.

Function Machines have 3 parts

IN ➡ FUNCTION ➡ OUT

IN - A number that goes into the machine
OUT - A number that comes out of the machine
FUNCTION - The calculation that the machine does.

Speed = $\dfrac{\text{Distance}}{\text{Time}}$

Always change minutes into hours

The **HINTS** are there to help you to understand measurements...have a look.

SKIPS™ CHALLENGE TIME!

Well Done! Now copy the numbers from the coloured boxes in the crossmaths into the matching coloured boxes below and answer the following questions:

Miss Joy Driver travels for ☐☐ minutes, at a speed of ☐☐ km/h.

Then stops for a break for ☐☐ minutes before continuing her journey at ☐☐ km/h for ☐ hours.

A) What is the total distance travelled by Miss Joy Driver? = ☐ _ _ _ km

B) What is the average speed she travelled at? = ☐ _ _ km/h

That's great

MEASUREMENTS

ACROSS

2 20 mm = ? cm
3 4cm = ? mm
4 2cm = ? mm
7 6Kg = ? g
8 7cm = ? mm
10 50mm = ? cm
11 9.70m = ? cm
13 400cm = ? m
14 2cm = ? mm
15 11000mm = ? m
21 0.103L = ? ml
24 How long will it take to travel 49 km at 7km/h?
26 In how many hours from 19:00 will it be midnight?
27 What is my speed if it takes me 11 hours to travel 99km?
28 How far will I go if I travel for 2 hours at 8km/h?
30 How far will I go if I travel at 5km/h for 6 hours?

A train travels at a speed of 20 km/h for 15 minutes. It then stops at a station for 25 minutes before continuing the journey for a further 10 minutes at a speed of 30km/h

31 What is the total distance travelled?
32 What was the total time for the whole journey?
33 What was the average speed?

DOWN

1 6m = ? cm
3 470cm = ? m
5 60mm = ? cm
6 6.392kg = ? g
9 920cm = ? m
12 1.8km = ? m
16 336cm = ? m
17 549cm = ? m
18 0.040L = ? ml
19 612cm = ? m
20 4.2cm = ? mm
22 How many hours are there in 720 minutes?
23 43mm = ? $\frac{1}{4}$ cm
25 What is $1\frac{1}{4}$ hours in minutes?
29 A car is travelling at a average speed of 75km/h. It takes 8 hours to travel from city A to city B. What is the distance between the two cities?

HINTS

To convert from one unit to another you have to use the following:

```
        ÷ 10              ÷ 100              ÷ 1000
    ────────────►     ────────────►     ────────────►
mm          cm    cm           m    m            km
```

```
        ×10               ×100               ×1000
    ◄────────────     ◄────────────     ◄────────────
mm          cm    cm           m    m            km
```

```
            ÷ 1000              ÷ 1000
        ────────────►       ────────────►
    g           kg    ml              L
```

```
            × 1000              × 1000
        ◄────────────       ◄────────────
    g           kg    ml              L
```

Speed = $\frac{\text{Distance}}{\text{Time}}$ i.e. S = $\frac{D}{T}$

Therefore D = S x T and T = $\frac{D}{S}$

(Remember algebra and the balancing method)

Always change minutes into hours when given a question. This is done by dividing the minutes by 60 e.g. 20 mins = $\frac{20}{60}$ = $\frac{1}{3}$ hrs

21

SECTION 2

Parallelogram - opposite angles are the same.

If scale on a map is 1 : 50,000. 1cm on map = 50,000 cms in real distance.

SKIPS™

SKIPS CHALLENGE TIME!

Well Done! Now copy the numbers from the appropriate coloured boxes in the crossmaths into the matching coloured boxes below and answer the following question:

Mr Don Key was ☐☐ **minutes late to catch a train which was due at the station**

at ☐☐:☐☐ **. At what time did he arrive at the station?** = ☐☐:☐☐

Brilliant

EXAM BASED 1

ACROSS

2 What is three thousand two hundred and nine in figures?

5 What is missing number?

4	8	12
8	?	16
12	16	20

6 Sacha is now twice his sister's age. In four years time Sacha will be 16. How old will his sister be then?

7 Helen is going on holiday which cost £180. Each week she pays £15 towards the cost. So far she has paid £75. How many more weekly payments does she need to make?

8 The perimeter of a rectangle is 18cm. If the longest side is 6cm, what is the area?

12 33 children are going on trip to Italy. The trip costs £25 each. How much money should be collected in total from all the children?

13 Which value does the 9 digit in 11,297 represent?

14 In a class of 32, three quarters like painting. How many do not like painting?

16 Dylan gets £2.50 in pocket money each week. His younger brother Shaan gets half as much. If Shaan saves all his pocket money for a year how much money will he have?

20 This machine divides by five and then multiplies by three. If 185 goes into the machine what number comes out?

21 Calculate $5^3 \times 2^2 \div 5$.

25 Rishi and Sacha held a book sale at school, they sold 48 large books at 10p each and 65 small books at 5p each. How much money did they raise at their sale? (Answer in pounds and pence).

26 Nicole's mum buys her a new longer skirt in a sale at half price. The original cost of the skirt was £9.50. How much change did Nicole's mum get from a £10 note? (Answer in pounds and pence).

27 A rectangle has an area of 54cm². If two of the sides are both 6cm long, what is the length of each of the other two sides?

28 Write 6.528424 to two decimal places.

DOWN

1 A box holds 38 cups. How many boxes will be needed to hold 646 cups?

3 525 raffle tickets were sold by 25 pupils in one school. On average how many tickets did each pupil sell?

4 Nicole draws a plan of her house using a scale of 1cm to 50m. On the plan the garden is 6cm long. What is the real length of the garden in metres?

9 What number does the arrow point to?

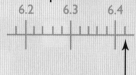

10 A map of Spain is drawn to scale of 1:750,000. What real distance is represented by 1cm on the map in kilometres?

11 In the parallelogram angle y measures 110°. What is the size of angle x?

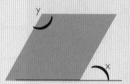

15 The W.B.A football magazine has 56 pages. $\frac{2}{7}$ of the pages contain typing errors. How many pages contain typing errors?

17 $3a + 7b - 4c = x$. If $a = 6$, $b = 5$, and $c = 8$, what is the value of x?

18 An isosceles triangle has angles x, y, and z. Angle x measures 55°. Angles x and y differ in size by 15°. What is the angle of z?

19 What is the perimeter of the shape? (not to scale).

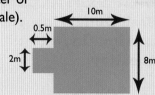

22 The ratio of cars to vans on a car park is 26:3. If there are 81 vans in the car park how many cars are there?

23 From the following, which number is exactly divisible by both 2 and 8, 18, 28, 32, 42, 52,

24 A map of Holland is drawn to a scale of 1:400,000. What real distance is represented by 1cm on the map in Km?

23

www.skipscrosswords.co.uk

SKIPS CHALLENGE TIME!

Well Done! Now copy the numbers from the appropriate coloured boxes in the crossmaths, into the matching coloured boxes below and answer the following question:

Miss Lilly Pond is ▢/▢ of Mrs Rose Bush's age, but ▢ years older than Miss Ivy Plant.

If Mrs Rose Bush is ▢▢ , how old is Miss Ivy Plant? = ▢

www.skipscrosswords.co.uk

EXAM BASED 2

ACROSS

1 What is the range of these weights 1.2Kg, 1.1Kg, 1.05Kg, 1.4Kg, 1.25Kg?

2 Which one of these decimal numbers is the largest 2.89, 2.98, 2.08, 2.9, 2.0?

5 What is the answer when 800 is divided by 5?

6 What percentage of the shape is shaded in?

9 Eggs are packed into boxes of nine. How many full boxes can be packed when there are one hundred and ten eggs in total?

11 What comes out of this machine?

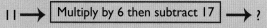

11 ⟶ | Multiply by 6 then subtract 17 | ⟶ ?

13 The mean of five numbers is 7. Three of the five numbers are 5,10,and 12. The other two numbers are the same. What is the value of these numbers?

16 What is the value of x in the following equation: $4x + 6 = 8x - 6$?

17 What is four out of twenty as a percentage?

18 What is the missing angle?

19 Which number is exactly divisible by 9 and 12 out of the following; 306, 198, 321, 252, 228?

20 How many times does 4 go into 560?

26 A bottle of water costs £1.15 and ice-creams costs 80p each. How much will it cost to buy 5 bottles of water and four ice-cream's? (Answer in pounds and pence).

27 A picture costing £12.50 is reduced by 30% in a sale. What is the sale price of the picture? (Answer in pounds and pence)

DOWN

2 A bag contains 200 marbles. 10% of the marbles are red and the rest are blue. How many red marbles are in the bag?

3 Hexley uses his mobile phone to send text messages. Each text costs 5p and he sends 60 messages a week. How much does he spend on text messages a week? (Answer in pence).

4 178 people get onto a train. At the next stop 59 more people get on the train, whilst 67 people get off. How many people are now on the train?

5 $5x + 3y - z = t$. If $x = 2$, $y = 5$ and $z = 10$. What is the value of t?

7 Emma and Nicole share 960 sweets between them in the ratio 5:3. How many more sweets does Emma get than Nicole?

8 What is the Median of this set of numbers: 8, 9, 5, 5, 2, 6, 2, 3, 6?

10 What is the missing angle from this right angle triangle? x =

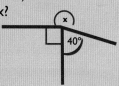

12 What is 11% of £420? (Answer in pounds and pence)

14 What is the missing angle x?

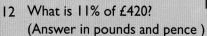

15 Shiv is saving to buy Glen Hoddle footy boots costing £85. He saves £6.50 a week and already has £27 in savings. How many more weeks will he have to save before he has enough money to buy the boots?

21 Write thirteen thousand and forty five.

22 What is 4% of £5? (Answer in pence)

23 Find the difference between 8 + 8 + 8 + 8 and 8 times 6.

24 This function machine squares a number then subtracts 45 from it. What comes out?

12 ⟶ | FUNCTION | ⟶ ?

25 If 20% of my money is 40p. How much do I have altogether? (Answer in pounds)

MEDIAN
Arrange numbers in size order. It is the middle number.

All angles on a pie chart add up to 360°

SKIPS™

SKIPS CHALLENGE TIME!
Well Done! Now copy the numbers from the appropriate coloured boxes in the crossmaths, into the matching coloured boxes below and answer the following question:

Mr Jack Pot has £ ☐ . He spends ☐/☐ of it and then gives £ ☐.☐☐ to his friend Robin Banks.

How much does he have left? = £ _____

That's great

26

www.skipscrosswords.co.uk

ACROSS

2   What is the value of the digit 8 in 98760?

3   If $6x - 15 = 4x + 5$ what is the value of x?

Here is a plan of a room

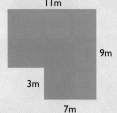

4   How far is it all the way around the edge of the room?

5   How much area of carpet is required to cover the room?

10   Write 181.879 to one decimal place.

11   Write 171.664 to two decimal places.

13   If $5x + 9 = 54 - 4x$ what is the value of x?

15   The function of the machine is to multiply by four and then add twelve.
What is the value of x?

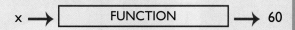

20   What is the square root of 64?

21   Convert 1604mm into cm's.

22   On a pie chart what is the angle of a slice if it cut into three equal slices?

A full packet of salt contains 600gms. From a 3.5kg container of loose salt answer the following:

23   How many full packets of salt can be made?

24   How many grams are left over?

25   What is the measurement of 0.351 litres in millilitres?

DOWN

1   A large container can hold 7 litres of water. How many containers can be filled completely with 144 litres of water?

3   If $6y - 12 = 4y + 22$. What is the value of y?

4   Books cost £3.99 at a store and the school buys 125 of them. What is the total cost?

6   400 children walk past the West Bromwich Albion football stadium in one hour. $\frac{1}{5}$ of them are girls. How many of them are boys?

7   In 2007 there were 43 members in drama club. In 2008 there were 12 new members. In 2009 there were 6 new members and 7 members who left. In 2010 there were 6 new members and 9 members who left. In 2011 there were only 3 new members. How many members were there in 2011 drama club?

8   What number does the arrow point to?

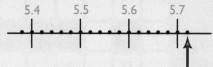

9   Rachael goes to the library to return 4 books. They are all overdue by one week so she has to pay four fines. From one pound she gets 16p change. How much is the fine on each book?

12   What is the value of the digit 6 in the number 18,640?

14   From the survey of 110 children how many boys gave dance as their favourite music?

FAVOURITE MUSIC

	DISCO	DANCE	CLASSICAL
BOYS	31	?	11
GIRLS	13	19	15

16   What is the median of the following set of numbers: 3, 6, 3, 14, 11, 8, 3?

17   What is the value of the unit in the following number: 892.421?

18   Dylan has 30 semi-detached properties and 10 detached properties. What fraction of his properties are semi-detached?

19   Write this improper fraction as a decimal $\frac{16}{10}$.

SKIPS CHALLENGE TIME!

Well Done! Now copy the numbers from the appropriate coloured boxes in the crossmaths, into the matching coloured boxes below and answer the following questions:

Barry Schmelly's bedroom is ☐ . ☐ ☐ metres long and ☐ . ☐ metres wide.

A) What is the perimeter of his room? = ☐☐☐ . ☐☐ m

B) How much carpet does he need to cover the entire floor?

= ☐☐☐ . ☐☐☐☐ m² *That's great*

28

www.skipscrosswords.co.uk

EXAM BASED 4

ACROSS

1   What is the missing angle x on this Isosceles triangle? x =

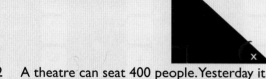

2   A theatre can seat 400 people. Yesterday it was $\frac{11}{20}$ full. How many seats were full?

5   It costs £500 to hire a car for a week. A 5% deposit is paid when booking. How much is this deposit?

6   Convert 0.625 litres into millilitres.

11   The temperature inside the house is 40 degrees higher than it is outside. If the temperature outside is − 7 degrees, what is the temperature inside?

12   If the area of a triangle is 6cm² and its base length is 4cm, what is its height?

14   Work out $\frac{2}{5} - \frac{6}{20}$

15   Work out $1\frac{1}{2} \div 1\frac{2}{3}$

16   What is the mode of these set of numbers: 14, 17, 15, 15, 14, 17, 21, 17?

19   A model car 5cm long is made to a scale 1 : 43. What is the length of the real car in cm?

20   Round to two decimal places the number 55.494.

21   What is seventeen point nine, minus six point six seven?

22   What is the area of a rectangle which has a length of 113cm and a perimeter of 234cm?

23   What value does the 5 represent in 15024?

24   Ben eats two thirds of a tin of beans every day. How many tins will he finish in 18 days?

DOWN

1   Convert 460mm into cm's.

3   What is x if 4x + 2 = 74?

4   You pay a 8% deposit when booking a holiday. If the total cost is £875. How much is the deposit?

7   An adult train ticket cost £20.49 each and a child ticket cost £18.59 each. What is the total cost if 3 adults and 3 children catch the train?

8   What is seven squared?

9   What is the perimeter of a square which has a side length of 10m?

10   What is the volume of the cuboid shown?

13   Round this number to 2 decimal places 11.6251

17   How many minutes are there in three hours and four minutes?

18   What is the missing angle, x?

19   Write this improper fraction as a decimal $\frac{42}{20}$.

29

A percentage is out of 100

A Prime number only has two factors, 1 and itself

SKIPS CHALLENGE TIME!

Well Done! Now copy the numbers from the appropriate coloured boxes in the crossmaths, into the matching coloured boxes below and answer the following question:

Mr Lu Zer wishes to buy litres of paint. How much cheaper is it to buy

$2\frac{1}{2}$ - litre tins than [ ] one litre tins?

= £ ___ . ___ ___

SKIPS Paint $2\frac{1}{2}$ litres

SKIPS Paint 1 litre

£ [ ] . [ ] [ ]   £ [ ] . [ ] [ ]

30

www.skipscrosswords.co.uk

EXAM BASED 5

ACROSS

1   What value does the four digit represent in the number 14123?

2   What is 0.1146 when rounded to 2 decimal places?

5   Sacha and Rishi were helping to carry the shopping home. Sacha was carrying a 450g bag of potatoes and 2 bags of fruit each weighing 225g. The total weight of Rishi's bag was exactly half the total weight of Sacha's bag. How much did Rishi's bag weigh?

6   $3ab = 150$. If $b = 2$, what is the value of a?

7   What is the volume of a box which has measurements of length 7mm, height 3mm and width 6mm? (Write your answer in mm³)

9   What is the perimeter of a rectangle which has measurements of length 19cm and width 9cm?

18   What is the mean of the following numbers 220, 221, 229, 236, 239?

19   If $12a - 20 = 4a + 4$ what is the value of a?

20   This machine multiplies by 5 and the adds 5. If 50 comes out what number goes into the machine.

$$? \longrightarrow \boxed{\text{FUNCTION}} \longrightarrow 50$$

23   What do the angles on a straight line add up to?

24   What is the biggest angle in a right angle triangle?

26   Which number is incorrectly placed?

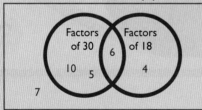

27   If the area of a triangle is 140cm² and its height is 10cm. How long is its base?

28   What is 13% of 400?

30   Calculate $3^3 - 2^2 - 2^3 = ?$

31   What is the value of the 2 digit in the number 12401?

32   Which number lies half way between 23 and 31?

34   10% of Viraaj's money is 90p. How much does he have in total? (Write your answer in pounds)

35   Write 120% as a decimal.

36   Convert 415cm into metres.

37   Convert 2600g into kg. Write your answer to 2 decimal places.

DOWN

1   Write 4.7774 to 2 decimal places.

3   There are 54 pupils in a class. $\frac{2}{9}$ travel to school by bus, $\frac{4}{9}$ travel by car. The rest walk. How many pupils walk to school?

4   Find the angle x.

8   How many hours are there in 1440 minutes?

10   How may equal sides does an equilateral triangle have?

11   What is the missing angle x?

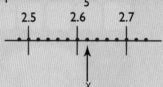

12   Write this improper fraction $\frac{56}{5}$ as a decimal.

13   What is x?

14   The pie chart shows how 44 children had their lessons at school today. How many did P.E?

Music 40%   English 10%

15   Lamb costs £3.50 per kilogram and fish costs £4.00 per kilogram. Mr Large buys 20kg of lamb and 10 kg of fish. How much does he spend? (Write your answer in pounds)

16   If $4x + 12 = 5x$ what is the value of x?

17   What is the median of this set of numbers: 25, 28, 31, 33, 19, 22, 23?

21   A deposit of 8% is required to book a hall for a party. If the hall costs £500 to book, how much deposit is required?

22   What is x?

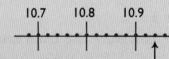

25   What is 64.5mm in cm's?

29   Which one of these is not a prime number: 5, 7, 9, 11, 17?

33   A frog drops to the bottom of a well 5m deep. It crawled up 3m each day but unfortunately slipped back 2 metres every night. How many days does it take for the frog to climb to the top?

31

The note bubbles in the puzzle read:

"All angles on a straight line add up to 180°"

"18 : 30 is the same time as 6.30pm on a 24 hour clock"

Grid symbols visible: + , = , x , − , ÷ , 5 , 3 , 0

SKIPS™

SKIPS CHALLENGE TIME!

Well Done! Now copy the numbers from the appropriate coloured boxes in the crossmaths, into the matching coloured boxes below and answer the following question:

Mr Tim Burr the train driver was ☐☐ minutes late with his train.

He arrived at ☐ minutes after midnight.

When was it due according to the 24 hour clock? = ___ ___ : ___ ___

That's great

ACROSS

1 Write in figures nine thousand, six hundred and forty five.

2 Write in figures ninety six thousand, five hundred and twenty three.

5 Fifteen lots of three and two lots of four equals?

6 What is the missing angle?

7 What is the value of the digit 9 in the number 1194?

10 If we double this number and add 10 the answer is 400. What is this number?

11 If we add 3 and then add another 3 the answer is 21. What is the number we started with?

15 If $3x - 10 = x$, what is x?

18 What is the missing angle?

23 There is a sale in a game store. The sign says 25% off. Den buys a game that originally costs £24. How much change does Den get from £20?

25 Joe has £200 to spend on his birthday party. If party bags cost £5 each and food is £2 each how many children including himself can go to the party and have both food and a party bag?

27 There are 3600 coloured ice lollies in a freezer of 4 different colours. The amount of each of the colours is shown. How many ice lollies are green?

28 A car weighs 1430kg when full with passengers. If the passengers weigh $\frac{2}{5}$ of the total weight, how much does the car weigh without the passengers inside?

29 Look at the parallelogram and calculate angle x.

30 Mark set out from school at 3.30pm, goes to his grandma's and eventually gets home at 19.49. How many minutes after he left school did he arrive home?

DOWN

Change the order of the figures in the following numbers to make the second largest number possible.

1 9009.

3 33624.

4 What is the value of 4^5?

8 What is the value of the digit of 9 in the number 11943?

9 12 is 3 more than half this number. What is this number?

10 Write in figures nineteen thousand two hundred and twelve.

12 Write as a fraction 0.6.

13 This number is 2 less than half of 20.

14 Write as a fraction 0.5.

16 Write as a fraction 0.05.

17 What is 75% as a fraction?

19 What is the missing angle?

20 Calculate $\frac{5}{8}$ of 96.

21 Write in figures six thousand nine hundred and eighty nine.

22 What is the square root of 100?

24 Write in figures fifty four thousand eight hundred and twenty one.

25 A thermometer reads 27 degrees. If the temperature drops by 3 degrees every 2 hours, how long would it take for the temperature to reach −9 degrees?

26 Sharon measures her stride. It is 85cm. If she takes 200 strides, how many metres has she gone?

31 What is the perimeter of the shape shown?

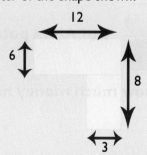

33

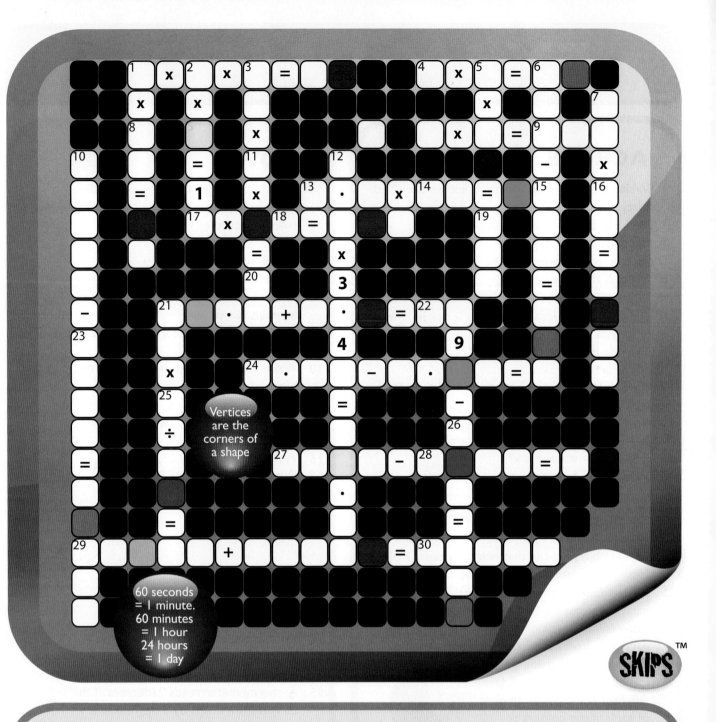

Vertices are the corners of a shape

60 seconds = 1 minute. 60 minutes = 1 hour 24 hours = 1 day

SKIPS™

SKIPS CHALLENGE TIME!

Well Done! Now copy the numbers from the appropriate coloured boxes in the crossmaths, into the matching coloured boxes below and answer the following question:

[ ] / [ ] 's of Anita potty's money is [ ] [ ] p.

How much money has she altogether? = [ ] p

34

EXAM BASED 7

ACROSS

1   How many faces does a cube have?
2   How many faces does a cylinder have?
4   How many edges does a square based pyramid have?
5   How many vertices does a triangular based pyramid have?
9   If a boy stands facing north and turns 60 degrees to his right, how much in angles does he need to continue turning right to get back to facing north again?
13 Convert 45mm into cm.
14 If $2y + 12 = 5y - 36$, what is the value of y?
17 How many sides does an octagon have?
18 How many vertices does a cylinder have?
21 What is the next highest prime number after 10?
22 What is the square root of 169?
24 What is the reading x?

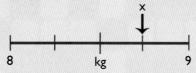

27 Convert 4.06kg to grams.
28 Write in figures three thousand nine hundred and eighty five.
29 Write thirty one thousand three hundred and thirty one.
30 What is the product of 2837 and 15?

DOWN

3   How many edges does a cuboid have?
6   What is the volume of a cube with an edge that measures 7cm?
7   Reduce the value of ninety two by twelve.
8   A man walks 1.4km to work everyday and at the end of the day walks back home again. How many kilometres does the man walk in an normal 5 day working week?
10 When opened, a tap lets 100ml of water through every second. If the tap is open for 2.5 minutes, how much water passes through in millilitres?
11 How many faces does a sphere have?
12 Convert 76mm into cm.
15 What is the volume of the cube which has this net?

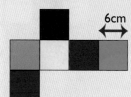

16 Mrs Flower gets to the cinema at 17:30. The film starts at 18:25. How long must she wait before the film starts?
19 A cube has a volume of 1000cm³. What is the area of each face?
20 This machine function is to square the number then add 60. If the number 6 goes in, what value comes out?

6 → [FUNCTION] → ?

21 How many minutes is one fifth of an hour?
23 How many seconds in 45 minutes?
25 Which figure in the number below has a value of thousands 15424?
26 What is the missing angle x?

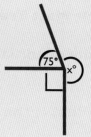

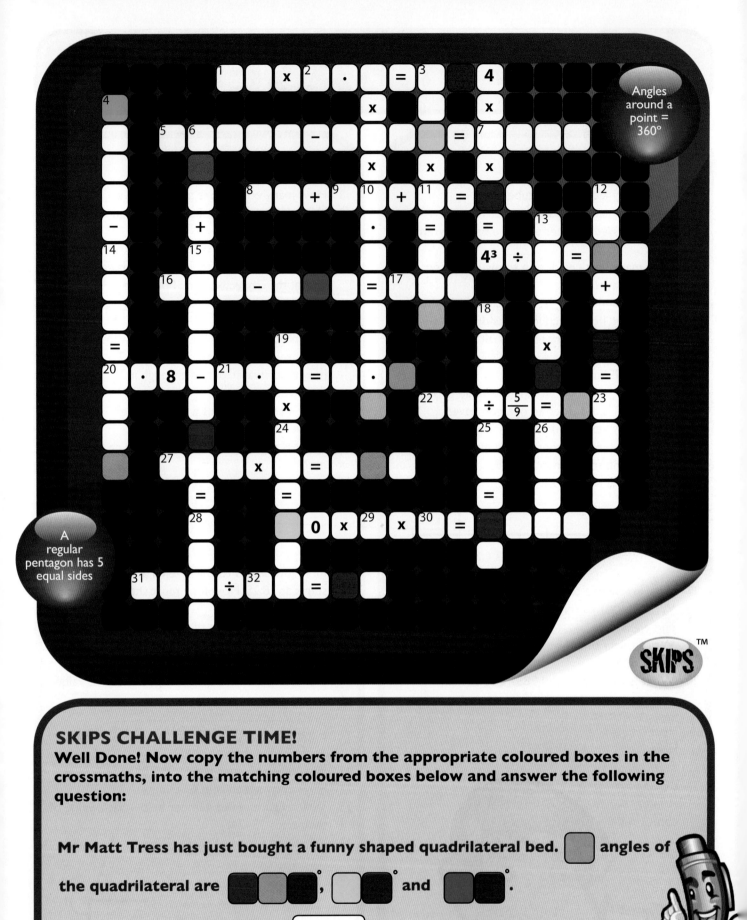

SKIPS CHALLENGE TIME!

Well Done! Now copy the numbers from the appropriate coloured boxes in the crossmaths, into the matching coloured boxes below and answer the following question:

Mr Matt Tress has just bought a funny shaped quadrilateral bed. ☐ angles of

the quadrilateral are ☐☐☐°, ☐☐° and ☐☐°.

What is the fourth angle? = ☐°

EXAM BASED 8

ACROSS

1 What is the perimeter of the shape shown?

12cm
6cm
8cm
3cm

2 A regular pentagon has a perimeter of 18cm. What is the length of each side of the pentagon ___cm?

5 Write in figures thirteen thousand five hundred and forty.

7 Calculate 127 x 33 = ?

8 Find the median of these numbers: 24, 18, 19, 28, 30, 9, 43, 57, 16, 22, 1

9 What is the median of these numbers: 25, 11, 12, 18, 26, 34, 21?

16 A rectangle has one side length of 10cm. Its perimeter is 100cm. What is the area of the rectangle?

17 What is the missing angle?

The following bar line graph shows how high children can jump

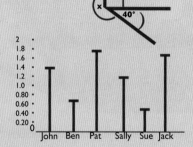

20 How high did Pat jump?

21 How high did Sue jump?

22 This function machine squares the number and then adds it to the product of 18 and 2. If number 3 goes into the machine what number comes out?

27 Two of the three angles of a triangle measure 35° and 44°, what is the size of the third angle?

29 Hema has three times more sweets than Shivam. If their dad gives them 16 sweets to share, how many sweets does Shivam get?

30 $3\frac{2}{5}$ add $1\frac{3}{5}$ =?

31 0.9 Litres = ___ ml?

32 If Thomas travels 5km in 20 minutes, how far would he have travelled in 3 hours and 20 minutes?

DOWN

3 What is the area of the isosceles triangle shown?

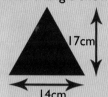

17cm
14cm

The bar graph below shows the amount of money a store took in one week.

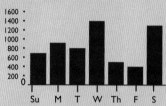

4 How much money did the shop take at the weekend?

14 How much money did the shop take on Monday?

6 What do the angles inside a quadrilateral shape always add up to?

10 Calculate 3.8 – 2.2 =.

11 From the spinner, which number is more likely to come up?

12 Calculate 9.93m = ___ cm.

13 How many minutes are there in 20 hrs 50 mins?

15 Calculate 15% of 7200.

18 From the diagram shown what is the missing angle x?

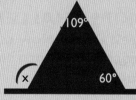

109°
x
60°

19 Calculate 0.75 x 10 x 10.

23 Calculate 1.008 x 10³.

24 What is the mode of this list of numbers: 12, 14, 9, 14, 12, 12, 9, 15, 18, 4?

25 If 3x + 22 = 5x – 4, what is x?

26 What value does the digit 5 have in the number 35021?

28 What value does the digit 1 represent in 21222?

Obtuse angles are greater than 90° but less than 180°

Acute angles are greater than 0° but less than 90°

SKIPS ™

SKIPS CHALLENGE TIME!

Well Done! Now copy the numbers from the appropriate coloured boxes in the crossmaths, into the matching coloured boxes below and answer the following question:

Annie Body buys packets of sweets that cost p.

She then re-sells them at 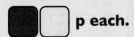 p each.

How much profit will she make if she sells 200 packets? = £  _ _ . _ _

That's great

ACROSS

1 What is the perimeter of a regular pentagon that has a side length of 75cm?

2 What is the value of the digit 2 in the number 1298?

7 Round this number to the nearest ten: 1555

8 What is 10^3?

12 Reduce 110 by 24.

14 What is 43 less than 5 x 9?

15 Calculate 1.067×10^3

16 Round this number to the nearest ten: 665.

18 The temperature in a fridge is – 4 Celcius. When the fridge is turned off the temperature rises 3 Celcius every hour. What is the temperature in the fridge 4 hours after it is turned off?

In a theatre there are 200 adults and children. There is one adult for every 3 children.

19 How many children are there?

21 How many adults are there?

24 A boy is 8 years older than his sister. How old is his sister when he is 3 times older than her?

25 A box can hold 8 dvds. If there is a total of 87 dvds how many complete boxes would it fill?

DOWN

2 Convert 20km into metres.

3 Which of these numbers is the smallest: 20.91, 20.71, 24.21, 20.01, 24.3?

4 Which of these numbers is the biggest: 40,442, 40,017, 5,986, 49984, 40631?

5 What is x?

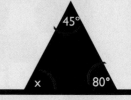

6 Round this number to the nearest thousand: 29,537.

9 If a = 9, b = 2a, and c = b – a. What is the value of c if a is doubled?

10 Which of these is an acute angle: 186°, 90°, 270°, 84°?

11 Which one of these decimal numbers is the smallest: 4.19, 4.28, 4.03, 4.09, 4.099?

13 Which one of these numbers is the largest: 10,379, 10,018, 11,111, 9,984, 10,306?

16 What is the cost of 20 metres of copper at £15.00 per half metre?

17 How many minutes are there is 11 hours and 40 minutes?

20 Take one from 17 and divide by eight.

22 Miss Jones started the journey to the USA at 11.45am. She arrived at 22.12. How long did the journey take in minutes?

23 Calculate 25% of 168.

39

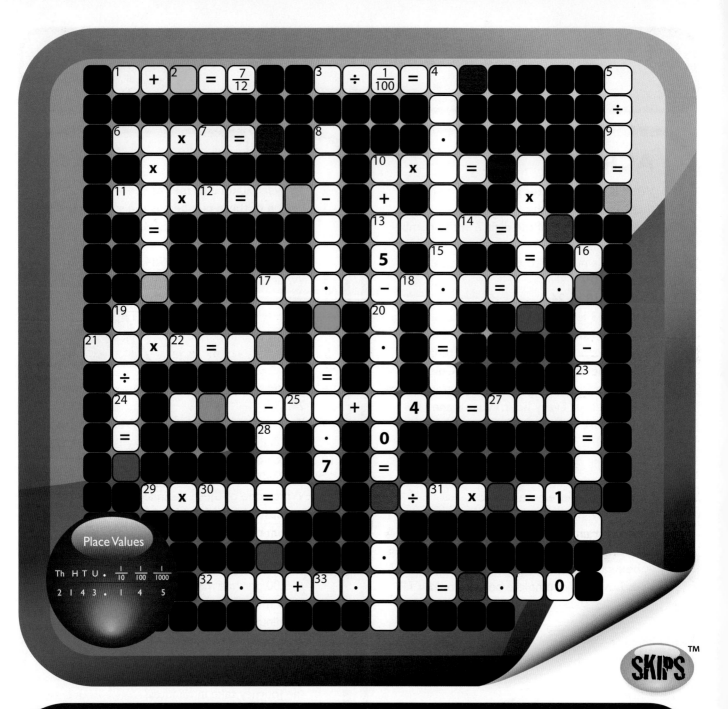

Place Values

Th	H	T	U	.	$\frac{1}{10}$	$\frac{1}{100}$	$\frac{1}{1000}$
2	1	4	3	.	1	4	5

SKIPS™

SKIPS CHALLENGE TIME!

Well Done! Now copy the numbers from the appropriate coloured boxes in the crossmaths, into the matching coloured boxes below and answer the following question:

Mr Bill Ding wants to build the thick wall shown below.

How many of these cube bricks ⬛ **would be needed to make the wall?**

⬛ 1cm

◻ cm   ◻ cm

◻ ◻ cm   = ◻◻◻ cube bricks

That's great

EXAM BASED 10

ACROSS

1. What fraction of this shape is shaded?

2. Which fraction below is similar to the decimal 0.33? $\frac{1}{2}$, $\frac{1}{4}$, $\frac{1}{3}$, $\frac{1}{5}$?

3. Write this decimal as a fraction 0.17.

6. Calculate $\frac{3}{7}$ of 56

7. Which one of these fractions is the smallest $\frac{1}{2}$, $\frac{2}{5}$, $\frac{6}{4}$, $\frac{8}{10}$, $\frac{1}{3}$, $\frac{7}{15}$?

11. Which one of these angles is acute 110°, 90°, 270°, 35°, 105°?

12. Calculate $\frac{5}{7}$ + $\frac{5}{14}$ − $\frac{3}{14}$ = ? (reduce to its lowest term).

13. Convert 640mm into centimetres.

14. A tank holds 520 litres of water. 40 litres of water is drained every minute when the plug is pulled out How many minutes will it take until the tank holds 200 litres?

17. What is 1040% as a decimal number?

18. Which is the largest number from the following: 8.03, 8.002, 8.2, 8.020, 8.022?

21. From the following function machine what number comes out?

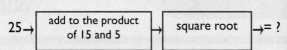

22. Which one of these is not a prime number: 2, 5, 1, 7, 11?

25. If 3b = 4a − c + 6 and b = 20, c = 30. What is the value of a?

27. Write in figures one thousand and fifty five.

29. How many factors does the number 16 have?

30. If 3a + 16 = 7², what is the value of a?

31. How many equal sides does a isosceles triangle have?

32. A baker has 6kg of flour. He needs 225g of flour to make each cake. If he makes 12 cakes, how much flour does he have left? (Answer in kg's).

33. Alice went shopping and spent £8.90 on food, £2.50 on socks and £15.00 on a hat. How much money did she have left out of £30.00?

DOWN

4. James is given $\frac{2}{7}$ share of some money. The amount he gets is £3.80 How much money was there before James got his share?

5. Which one of these fractions is the smallest: $\frac{5}{8}$, $\frac{4}{7}$, $\frac{1}{2}$, $\frac{17}{33}$, $\frac{11}{20}$?

8. What is one fifth of one hour in minutes?

9. What is this decimal as a fraction 0.875?

10. What value does the digit 5 have in 11405?

15. What is $\frac{3}{4}$ of 4.4 litres?

16. A jug holds 2200ml of orange. It takes 100 jugs of orange to fill a tank. How much orange does the tank hold if it is full? (Give the answer in litres).

17. What distance in km is covered if a coach travels at 80km/h for 20 hours?

19. What is the volume of a box that has measurements length 4cm height 4cm width 2.5cm?

20. Convert 7350g into kg.

23. What is the area of a triangle that has height of 13cm and a base length of 10cm?

24. A liquid freezes at −16 degrees. Some of the frozen liquid is heated up by 6 degrees every thirty minutes. What is the temperature of the liquid after 2 hours of heating?

28. There are 92 chocolates in a tin, one quarter are soft centred the rest are hard centred. How many are hard centred?

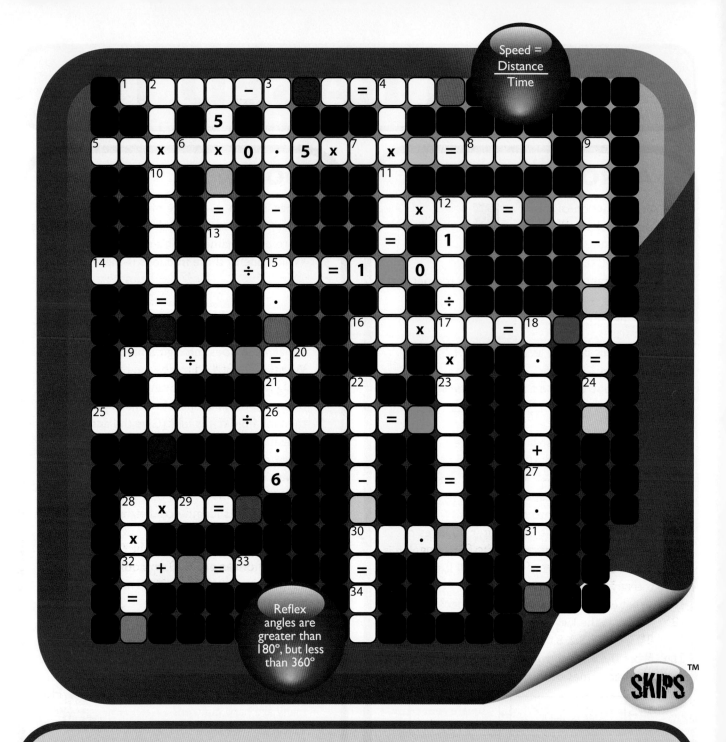

Speed = Distance / Time

Reflex angles are greater than 180°, but less than 360°

SKIPS™

SKIPS CHALLENGE TIME!

Well Done! Now copy the numbers from the appropriate coloured boxes in the crossmaths, into the matching coloured boxes below and answer the following question:

Monday to Friday Tish Hughes starts school at ☐ . ☐☐ am and

finishes at ☐ . ☐☐ pm.

She has a ☐ hour lunch break.

How long is she in lessons each week? = [____] hours [____] minutes

Well Done

EXAM BASED11

ACROSS

1 A show has 54 rows of seats. There are 28 seats in each row. How many people can have seats during the show?

3 A box of matches has 35 match sticks in it. There are 24 boxes in the store. How many matchsticks are there altogether?

5 The area of a triangle is 25mm², if the height of the triangle is 5mm what is the base length?

6 Which digit in the following number has a value of tenths 23.54?

7 The boy to girls ratio is 2 : 3. If there are 6 girls, how many boys are there?

8 What value does the digit 3 represent in the number 9364.21?

12 Write the following fraction as a percentage $\frac{3}{12}$

14 Write eleven thousand and sixty in digits.

15 Which one is not a factor of 88:
4, 22, 2, 10, 8?

16 Calculate $\frac{4}{9}$ of £63.

17 Work out the value of y in the following equation: 157 − y = 88.

19 What is the missing angle on a trapezium that has 3 inside angles of: 122°, 65° and 85°?

25 What is the value of the digit 1 in the number 19,007?

26 Round the following number to the nearest hundred 951.

28 Convert 0.6 into a fraction.

29 Write 62.5% as a fraction in its lowest term.

30 Convert 3469cm into metres.

32 Write 50% as a fraction in its lowest term.

DOWN

2 There are 464 players at a football tournament. The teams are made up of 8 players each. How many teams are there altogether?

3 Mr Large weighs 92kg and decides to go on a diet. He loses 10% of his weight. What is his new weight?

4 Shiv has ten 2 litres of pop for his party. A cup of pop holds 300ml. How many full cups of pop will Shiv have?

9 Which one of these angles is a reflex angle: 45, 112, 230, 175, 90?

10 Due to more people wanting to watch WBA play football, the length of the road outside had to be increased by 25%. The road was 800 metres long. How long is the road now in metres?

11 What is five percent of four hundred and eighty?

13 Mrs Jude started a telephone conversation at 10.30am. She talked until 13:50. How many minutes was she on the telephone?

18 Sarah went shopping and spent £12.60 on food, £5.50 on drinks and £10 on books. How much did she have left out of £30?

20 If the time is now 16:00 hours. In how many more hours will it be midnight?

21 Convert the following 716mm = cm.

22 From the diagram shown below what is the missing angle?

23 A cube has a volume of 1000cm³, what is the area of each face?

24 What is the mode of the following set of numbers: 91, 97, 94, 97, 92, 96, 97, 91?

27 How many vertices does a cylinder have?

31 How many faces does a sphere have?

33 How many edges does a cone have?

34 Write the following decimal as a percentage 0.70.

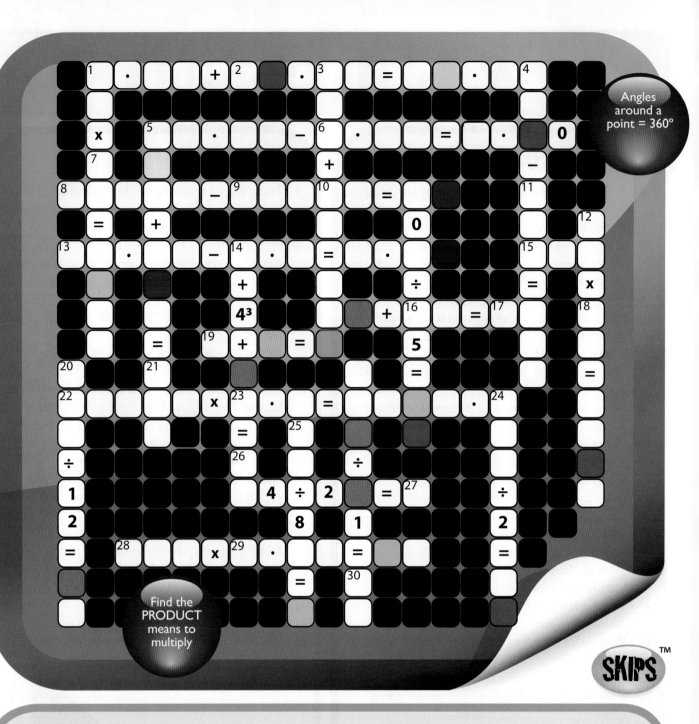

Angles around a point = 360°

Find the PRODUCT means to multiply

SKIPS CHALLENGE TIME!

Well Done! Now copy the numbers from the appropriate coloured boxes in the crossmaths, into the matching coloured boxes below and answer the following question:

Phil Graves bought a spade for work that was advertised for ☐☐ % off the normal selling price of £ ☐☐ .

When he went to pay he found out that the handle was faulty and so the shopkeeper dropped the price by a further ☐ % of the selling price.

How much did Phil Graves pay for the spade? = £ _____

That's great

44

ACROSS

1 Stan has one £2 coin, five 50p coins, one 20p coin, three 10p coins and a 5p coin. How much money does he have? (Answer in pounds and pence)

2 The monthly cost of house insurance has been reduced by 40%. The original cost was £38.50. How much does it cost now?

5 On a train journey children may travel half price. How much does it cost altogether for Mr and Mrs Butt and their 3 children to travel if an adult fare cost £3?

6 A £10 coat is reduced in a sale by 5%. What is its new price now?

8 Write in figures eighteen thousand seven hundred and two.

9 Calculate 444 x 42.

12 Which digit has a value of hundredths in 10.126?

13 Convert 1325cm = m.

14 What is the total weight of six parcels weighing 700g each? (Answer in kg.)

15 What is the value of 6 in the number 1642.21?

16 If $3r - 5 = 8^2$, what is the value of r?

17 What is $\frac{3}{7}$ ths of 126 = ?

19 How many seven-a-side netball teams can be made from 35 children?

22 Write in figures twenty one thousand two hundred and one.

23 Write 10% as a decimal.

28 What value does the digit 1 in the following represent 3102.24?

29 Which one of these is the largest number 0.989, 0.99, 0.909, 0.979?

DOWN

1 If you halve Barry's age and then add 4 the answer is 33. How old is Barry?

3 There are 432 seats at a theatre. 26 seats are given to staff. 217 have been sold already, the rest of the seats are available to buy. How many are available to buy?

4 What is the area of the shape shown?

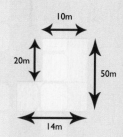

5 Add thirty two to the product of 4 and 32.

7 In a new restaurant, four chairs are needed for every table. If there are 17 tables, how many chairs are required?

10 If I travel 8km in 10 minutes, how far will I go in one hour?

11 Which one is an obtuse angle from the following: 270°, 45°, 89°, 136°, 184°?

What is the missing angle?

18 x = ?

20 y = ?

21 What is the volume of a box with measurements length 20m, height 8m and width 2.5m?

From the diagram what is the following?

24 Area = ?

25 Perimeter = ?

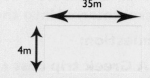

26 Double the difference between 49 and 88.

27 How many right angles turns are in a full 360 degrees turn?

30 Calculate the square root of 121.

If scale on a map is 1 : 50,000. 1cm on map = 50,000 cms in real distance.
SUM means to add

SKIPS

SKIPS CHALLENGE TIME!

Well Done! Now copy the numbers from the appropriate coloured boxes in the crossmaths, into the matching coloured boxes below and answer the following question:

A Greek trip cost £ ☐☐☐ per person. There is a £ ☐☐ reduction for each child.

How much would it cost for Mrs Holly Day to go with her husband and ☐ children for a Greek trip?

= £ _ _ _ _

Well Done

EXAM BASED 13

ACROSS

1 Which one of these angles is an obtuse 197, 120, 270, 181, 89?

3 Convert 975cm into metres.

6 This machine multiplies by 5 and then adds 1 Which number has been put into the machine.

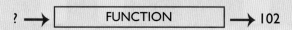

? → | FUNCTION | → 102

7 How many centimetres are there in 102mm.

8 Write in figures eighteen thousand two hundred and twenty two.

10 Write in figures eight thousand two hundred and twenty two.

11 What is the volume of a box that has measurements length 25m, height 20m and width 19.8m

17 Write in figures fifteen thousand five hundred and twenty six.

18 What is 1.059kg in grams?

21 A farmer has a field which has a length of 80 metres and width of 76 metres. What length of fencing does he require to go around the perimeter of the field?

22 Here is a sequence: 17, 15, 20, 18, 23, 21. What is the next number?

24 How many equal angles does an equilateral triangle have?

25 If x = 4 and y = 3, calculate 3(x + 2y).

28 What is the area of the shape shown?

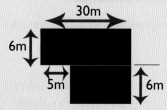

29 Divide the product of 18 and 5 by 6.

33 What is $\frac{1}{5}$ of 105905?

35 Write in decimal thirty one thousand one hundred and eleven.

DOWN

2 Which of these numbers is exactly divisible by 2 and 11. 4, 8, 11, 22, 36, 55?

3 What value does the digit 9 have in 18942

4 What is the sum of 34mm, 56mm and 26mm. (Answer in cm's).

5 What is the size of an angle that is half a right angle

7 What is the missing angle?

9 How many $2\frac{1}{2}$ cm strips can be cut from a piece of card 50cm wide.

12 Nicole's fat cat weighs 7950 grams. What is the cat's weight in kilograms?

13 How many minutes in one and a half hours?

14 Dylan has 19 conkers, Sid has 12 conkers and Alex has 11 conkers. What is the average number of conkers for each child?

15 In a theatre 25% of the seats were empty, but 315 seats were taken. How many empty seats were there?

16 What is the difference between twelve dozen and fifty nine?

19 The sum of two numbers is 171. One number is 52. What is the other number?

20 Halve the product of twenty and five, then add three.

23 What is 2800 grams in Kg

26 Four brothers have a mean age of 10. Three of the brothers are aged 13, 10 and 5. What is the age of the other brother?

27 If a triangle has an area of 18cm² and a height of 4cm. What is its base length?

30 A map of Happy Town is drawn to scale of 1 : 20000. What real distance does 1cm on the map represent in kilometres?

31 If x² + 6 = 150, what is the value of x?

32 What number lies half way between 85 and 99.

34 Find the sum of 13, 21 and fifty five

36 32 girls are in a drama class. $\frac{1}{8}$ of the girls prefer to sing, $\frac{5}{8}$ prefer to dance. The rest like to act. How many of the girls like to act?

Range equals highest value minus lowest value

10% of 50 means:
$\frac{10}{100} \times 50 = 5$

SKIPS™

SKIPS CHALLENGE TIME!

Well Done! Now copy the numbers from the appropriate coloured boxes in the Crossmaths, into the matching coloured boxes below and answer the following question:

Joe King the milkman and Kris Mass the butcher deliver to the same house.

In a period of [ ][ ] days, Joe calls every second day and Kris every third day.

They meet at the house twice in the first [ ] days.

How many more times do they meet during the [ ] week period? = [ ]

48

EXAM BASED 14

ACROSS

1 Three quarters of Denise's savings is £712.50. How much money has she altogether?

2 Write 1% as a decimal.

6 Which number is exactly divisible by 7 and 21 from: 17, 27, 21, 41, 26?

8 What number lies half-way between 31 and 65?

12 The area of a rectangle is 2530 cm². It is 55cm wide. What is its perimeter?

13 What value does the digit one have in 22109?

15 There are 35 pupils in a class. $\frac{4}{7}$ travel to school by bus, $\frac{2}{7}$ travel by car and the rest travel by skate board. How many pupils skate board to school?

18 Andrew is three times older than his dog. In two years' time he will be 29. How old is his dog today?

19 Divide 2156 by 7.

20 Double the difference between (4 x 6) and fifteen lots of eight.

24 What is 0.498 kg in grams?

25 Highclare School needs to put a fence around its junior rectangular playground to keep the naughty children in. The playground measures length 110 metres and width 95 metres. How many metres of fencing is required to go all around the edge of the playground?

27 Subtract 43 from the product of 16 and 5.

28 Which number is both a square number and a cube number from: 4, 8, 27, 36, 64?

Look at the table below which shows how long train spotter Trevor had to wait for his train to take him to school over a period of one week.

	Mon	Tues	Wed	Thur	Fri
Mins	9	5	12	6	1

29 What is the range?

30 What is ten percent more than one thousand eight hundred and twenty?

31 How many equal angles does an isosceles triangle have?

32 What is the product of 25% of 68 and 2% of 250?

DOWN

1 Divide 9.10km by 10 and give your answer in metres.

2 Write 11% as a decimal.

3 Write in figures twelve thousand six hundred and forty four.

4 A chocolate bar has 20 pieces. Mrs Choky Chip eats 9 pieces. What percentage of the pieces is left?

5 7.7496 What is this number to two decimal places?

7 What is the missing angle marked x?

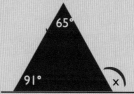

8 Mr Rodgers is buying some stationery for £43.20 Because he is spending over £30 he gets 10% reduction. How much discount does he get?

9 What is the next number in this sequence: 70 67 77 74 84

10 In a theatre $\frac{1}{5}$ of the seats were empty, however 680 were taken. How many empty seats were there?

11 What value does the digit 3 have in 13790?

12 Which angle below is an acute angle 92°, 113°, 270°, 25°, 179°?

14 There are 500 sheets of paper in a ream. How many sheets of paper are in 16 reams?

16 Take away eighteen-tenths from 112.4

17 What is $2\frac{3}{5}$ as a decimal?

21 A farmer plants 125 seeds in a tray. He puts the same number of seeds in each tray. If he uses 40 trays, how many seeds does he use altogether?

22 Divide 550 by 10².

23 What is the area of the shape shown?

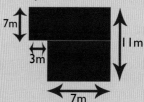

26 This machine multiplies by 12 and then subtracts 2. Which number has been put into the machine?

? → | FUNCTION | → 100

49

SECTION 3

Notes:

Page 3 NUMBERS

ACROSS		DOWN	
1	2	4	59
2	53	7	24
3	16	8	8
5	98	9	31
6	125	11	97
9	34	12	64
10	125	13	81
12	60	14	11
15	83	17	23
16	121	20	25
18	52	22	1
19	1	23	30
20	25	24	9
21	150		
25	39		
26	7		
27	24		
28	23		

SKIPS Challenge
64

8 2 7 9 7 6 8 0 1 1 2 6 4 7

Page 5 PLACE VALUE

ACROSS		DOWN	
1	6	1	616.1
2	0.1	3	1.90
4	406.55	4	40.65
5	310.06	5	352.01
10	5	6	5
11	45	7	5
13	8.35	8	4
15	5	9	117.32
16	1000	12	7
18	2.14	14	160.01
19	1.1	17	11
		20	1

SKIPS Challenge
A)65542 B)13459

6 3 4 5 1 9 5 4 5 2

Page 7 FRACTIONS

ACROSS		DOWN	
1	$\frac{5}{11}$	5	$\frac{4}{11}$
2	$\frac{4}{11}$	6	$\frac{11}{18}$
3	$\frac{4}{11}$	7	6
4	$\frac{23}{44}$	8	$\frac{5}{11}$
9	8	11	$\frac{2}{3}$
10	$\frac{2}{5}$	12	$\frac{1}{3}$
14	24	13	$\frac{9}{22}$
15	$\frac{1}{2}$	16	$\frac{3}{11}$
17	30	20	$\frac{1}{2}$
18	$\frac{3}{5}$	21	$\frac{4}{5}$
19	$\frac{1}{2}$	22	$\frac{1}{2}$
24	$\frac{1}{2}$	23	$\frac{17}{44}$
25	$\frac{5}{2}$		

SKIPS Challenge
A) $\frac{41}{44}$ B)2

9 1 $\frac{3}{11}$ 5 1 $\frac{39}{44}$ $\frac{9}{11}$ 2 3 $\frac{1}{2}$

Page 11 FRACTIONS, DECIMALS, PERCENTAGES

ACROSS		DOWN	
1	5	3	$\frac{3}{1000}$
2	$\frac{1}{20}$	4	0.001
		5	8.33
4	0.748	6	4
7	9	8	3
11	8	9	$\frac{3}{5}$
12	5		
13	8	10	0.70
14	2	17	4.7
15	40	18	20
16	12	19	0.18
17	4.2	21	1.2
20	1.1	22	10
23	8.6	24	0.7
25	$\frac{1}{2}$		
26	45		
27	9		

SKIPS Challenge
A)8.5 B)1.358

4 0 $\frac{1}{4}$ 8 2 1 6 5 3 7

Page 13 PERIMETERS, AREAS, COMPOUND SHAPES

ACROSS		DOWN	
1	4	1	44
2	4	2	40
3	24	3	28
4	32	5	64
6	6	8	32
7	9	9	8
8	30	10	100
17	42	11	2.5
18	88	12	81
19	8	13	10
22	16	14	36
24	32	15	144
25	48	16	180
27	38	18	80
28	8	20	12
29	54	21	92
30	62	22	10
		23	8
		24	38
		26	74

SKIPS Challenge
A)1440 B.1)19 B.2)456

6 7 5 2 8 0 1 4

Page 15 AVERAGES, RATIOS

ACROSS		DOWN	
1	11	2	99
2	9	3	10
6	6	4	6
7	8	5	15
8	5	10	70
9	15	11	10
13	20	12	55
14	125	15	60
17	45	16	15
24	25	18	18
25	15	19	19
26	3	20	4
27	14	21	5
28	24	22	35
29	39	23	7
32	9	30	6
33	100	31	70
34	25		

SKIPS Challenge
A)9 B)52

9 7 6 2 0 5 8 4 3

www.skipscrosswords.co.uk

Page 17 ANGLES

ACROSS		DOWN	
1	**45**	2	**55**
3	**80**	3	**80**
4	**75**	5	**55**
7	**65**	6	**110**
9	**55**	8	**55**
10	**24**	10	**25**
11	**75**	12	**95**
14	**161**	13	**215**
15	**228**	16	**180**
18	**12**	17	**130**
19	**3**		
20	**6**		
21	**3**		
22	$\frac{1}{8}$		
23	**45**		
24	**20**		
25	$\frac{3}{8}$		
26	**135**		
27	**60**		
28	$\frac{1}{4}$		
29	**90**		
30	**40**		
31	$\frac{1}{8}$		
32	**45**		
33	**20**		
34	$\frac{1}{8}$		
35	**45**		
36	**20**		

SKIPS Challenge
66

Tiles: 0, 7, $\frac{1}{4}$, 4, $\frac{3}{4}$, 9, 2, 6, 1, 3

Page 19 ALGEBRA

ACROSS		DOWN	
1	**3**	3	**4**
2	**6**	4	**36**
5	**6**	9	**4**
6	$\mathbf{10^2}$	12	$\mathbf{2^2}$
7	**4**	13	**12**
8	**15**	14	**3**
10	**36**	15	**18**
11	**31**	16	**9**
22	**144**	17	**85**
24	**5**	18	$\mathbf{5^2}$
25	**5**	19	**1**
26	**4**	20	**7**
31	$\mathbf{4^2}$	21	**50**
32	**8**	23	**42**
35	**25**	27	**8**
36	**600**	28	**15**
37	**9**	29	$\mathbf{6^2}$
38	**17**	30	**8**
39	**16**	33	**25**
		34	**27**

SKIPS Challenge
A)4 B)25

Tiles: 6, 1, 4, 7, 3, 0, 8, 5, 2

Page 21 MEASUREMENTS

ACROSS		DOWN	
2	**2**	1	**600**
3	**40**	3	**4.7**
4	**20**	5	**6**
7	**6000**	6	**6392**
8	**70**	9	**9.2**
10	**5**	12	**1800**
11	**970**	16	**3.36**
13	**4**	17	**5.49**
14	**20**	18	**40**
15	**11**	19	**6.12**
21	**103**	20	**42**
24	**7**	22	**12**
26	**5**	23	**4.3**
27	**9**	25	**75**
28	**16**	29	**600**
30	**30**		
31	**10**		
32	**50**		
33	**12**		

SKIPS Challenge
A)120 B)40

Tiles: 8, 6, 7, 2, 4, 3, 9, 5, 0

Page 23 EXAM BASED 1

ACROSS		DOWN	
2	3209	1	17
5	12	3	21
6	10	4	300
7	7	9	6.42
8	18	10	7.5
12	825	11	70
13	90	15	16
14	8	17	21
16	65	18	55
20	111	19	37
21	100	22	702
25	8.05	23	32
26	5.25	24	4
27	9		
28	6.53		

SKIPS Challenge
19 : 10

8
2
3
6
7
1
9
5
0
4

Page 25 EXAM BASED 2

ACROSS		DOWN	
1	0.35	2	20
2	2.98	3	300
5	160	4	170
6	40	5	15
9	12	7	240
11	49	8	5
13	4	10	50
16	3	12	46.20
17	20	14	230
18	32	15	9
19	252	21	13045
20	140	22	20
26	8.95	23	16
27	8.75	24	99
		25	2

SKIPS Challenge
7

2
7
4
3
0
1
9
8
6
5

Page 27 EXAM BASED 3

ACROSS		DOWN	
2	8000	1	20
3	10	3	17
4	40	4	498.75
5	87	6	320
10	181.9	7	54
11	171.66	8	5.72
13	5	9	21
15	12	12	600
20	8	14	21
21	160.4	16	6
22	120	17	2
23	5	18	$\frac{3}{4}$
24	500		
25	351	19	1.6

SKIPS Challenge
4.50

4
1
8
5
2
0
6
9
7
3

Page 29 EXAM BASED 4

ACROSS		DOWN	
1	45	1	46
2	220	3	18
5	25	4	70
6	625	7	117.24
11	33	8	49
12	$3\frac{1}{10}$	9	40
14	$\frac{9}{10}$	10	220
		13	11.63
15		17	184
		18	65
16	17	19	2.1
19	215		
20	55.49		
21	11.23		
22	452		
23	5000		
24	12		

SKIPS Challenge
A) 17.5 B) 17.875

6
3
5
4
2
7
9
1
0
8

Page 31 EXAM BASED 5

ACROSS		DOWN	
1	4000	1	4.78
2	0.11	3	18
5	450	4	48
6	25	8	24
7	126	10	3
9	56	11	110
18	229	12	11.2
19	3	13	2.62
20	9	14	11
23	180	15	110
24	90	16	12
26	4	17	25
27	28	21	40
28	52	22	10.94
30	15	25	6.45
31	2000	29	9
32	27	33	3
34	9		
35	1.2		
36	4.15		
37	2.60		

SKIPS Challenge
2.20

4
3
8
0
5
7
1
2
9
6

Page 33 EXAM BASED 6

ACROSS		DOWN	
1	9645	1	9090
2	96523	3	64323
5	53	4	1024
6	66	8	900
7	90	9	18
10	195	10	19212
11	15	12	$\frac{3}{5}$
15	5	13	$8\frac{1}{2}$
18	126	14	$1\frac{1}{20}$
23	2		
25	28	16	$\frac{3}{4}$
27	900		
28	858	17	
29	110		
30	259	19	212
		20	60
		21	6989
		22	10
		24	54821
		25	24
		26	170
		31	40

SKIPS Challenge
23 : 54

6
9
7
2
0
1
8
4
3
5

Page 35 EXAM BASED 7

ACROSS		DOWN	
1	6	3	12
2	3	6	343
4	8	7	80
5	4	8	14
9	300	10	15000
13	4.5	11	1
14	16	12	7.6
17	8	15	216
18	0	16	55
21	11	19	100
22	13	20	96
24	8.75	21	12
27	4060	23	2700
28	3985	25	5
29	31331	26	195
30	42555		

SKIPS Challenge
88

Code: 8 1 6 0 7 3 4 5 9 2

Page 37 EXAM BASED 8

ACROSS		DOWN	
1	40	3	119
2	3.6	4	2000
5	13540	14	900
7	4191	6	360
8	22	10	1.6
9	21	11	2
16	400	12	993
17	230	13	1250
20	1.8	15	1080
21	0.5	18	169
22	45	19	75
27	101	23	1008
29	4	24	12
30	5	25	13
31	900	26	5000
32	50	28	1000

SKIPS Challenge
85

Code: 4 9 6 2 0 8 1 5 7 3

Page 39 EXAM BASED 9

ACROSS		DOWN	
1	375	2	20000
2	200	3	20.01
7	1560	4	49984
8	1000	5	55
12	86	6	30000
14	2	9	18
15	1067	10	84
16	670	11	4.03
18	8	13	11111
19	150	16	600
21	50	17	700
24	4	20	2
25	10	22	627
		23	42

SKIPS Challenge
14.00

Code: 2 4 0 9 9 1 5 6 3 8 7

Page 41 EXAM BASED 10

ACROSS		DOWN	
1	$\frac{1}{4}$	4	13.30
2	$\frac{1}{3}$	5	$\frac{1}{2}$
3	$\frac{17}{100}$	8	12
6	24	9	$\frac{7}{8}$
7	$\frac{1}{3}$	10	5
11	35	15	3.3
12	$\frac{6}{7}$	16	220
13	64	17	1600
14	8	19	40
17	10.4	20	7.350
18	8.2	23	65
21	10	24	8
22	1	28	69
25	21		
27	1055		
29	5		
30	11		
31	2		
32	3.3		
33	3.60		

SKIPS Challenge
150

Code: 8 $\frac{1}{3}$ 6 2 $\frac{4}{7}$ 0 7 1 5 3

Page 43 EXAM BASED 11

ACROSS		DOWN	
1	1512	2	58
3	840	3	82.8
5	10	4	66
6	5	9	230
7	4	10	1000
8	300	11	24
12	25	13	200
14	11060	18	1.90
15	10	20	8
16	28	21	71.6
17	69	22	103
19	88	23	100
25	10000	24	97
26	1000	27	0
28	$\frac{3}{5}$	31	1
29	$\frac{5}{8}$	33	1
30	34.69	34	70
32	$\frac{1}{2}$		

SKIPS Challenge
27.30

Code: 4 $\frac{3}{10}$ 3 $\frac{3}{8}$ 1 7 8 6 0 9 2 $\frac{1}{2}$

Page 45 EXAM BASED 12

ACROSS		DOWN	
1	5.05	1	58
2	23.10	3	189
5	10.50	4	580
6	9.50	5	160
8	18702	7	68
9	18648	10	48
12	2	11	136
13	13.25	18	75
14	4.2	20	120
15	600	21	400
16	23	24	140
17	54	25	78
19	5	26	78
22	21201	27	4
23	0.1	30	11
28	100		
29	0.99		

SKIPS Challenge
48

Code: 4 6 9 0 7 8 2 5 3 1

Page 47 EXAM BASED 13

ACROSS		DOWN	
1	**120**	2	**22**
3	**9.75**	3	**900**
6	**20.2**	4	**11.6**
7	**10.2**	5	**45**
8	**18222**	7	**112**
10	**8222**	9	**20**
11	**9900**	12	**7.95**
17	**15526**	13	**90**
18	**1059**	14	**14**
21	**312**	15	**105**
22	**26**	16	**85**
24	**3**	19	**119**
25	**30**	20	**53**
28	**330**	23	**2.8**
29	**15**	26	**12**
33	**21181**	27	**9**
35	**31111**	30	**0.2**
		31	**12**
		32	**92**
		34	**89**
		36	**8**

SKIPS Challenge
1695

Numbered tiles: 4 5 1 7 0 2 9 3 6 8

Page 49 EXAM BASED 14

ACROSS		DOWN	
1	**950**	1	**910**
2	**0.01**	2	**0.11**
6	**21**	3	**12644**
8	**48**	4	**55**
12	**202**	5	**7.75**
13	**100**	7	**156**
15	**5**	8	**4.32**
18	**9**	9	**81**
19	**308**	10	**170**
20	**192**	11	**3000**
24	**498**	12	**25**
25	**410**	14	**8000**
27	**37**	16	**110.6**
28	**64**	17	**2.6**
29	**11**	21	**5000**
30	**2002**	22	**5.5**
31	**2**	23	**98**
32	**85**	26	**8.5**

SKIPS Challenge
3

Numbered tiles: 8 4 5 3 2 1 9 7

SECTION 4

SCRIBBLE PAD

SCRIBBLE PAD

www.skipscrosswords.co.uk